Georgie's TRUMP JARS

My son and I came up with this story on a car journey. We love coming up with silly, funny stories and now I think it's time to share them with the world.

First published in the UK in 2023
by Fiona Woodhead from FiandBooks.com
67 The Hollins, Triangle, Halifax, West Yorkshire. HX6 3LU.
www.fiandbooks.com

ISBN 978-1-909515-62-8

Copyright © 2023 by Lynsey Calvert
lcalvert1977@gmail.com
First edition printed November 2023
All rights reserved. Printed in the UK

Georgie has a secret that no one else knows.

Well, his cat Gizzie knows, but she keeps well away.

The secret is...

Georgie trumps into jars and keeps them hidden under his bed!

When a trump is brewing, he opens one of the jars, puts it near his bottom, trumps into it and then quickly puts the lid back on.

Every now and then, when he opens a jar, an old trump will sneak out.

THEY STINK.

His mum would go nuts if she knew.

Georgie thinks it is funny.

Gizzie, not so much.

"Hi Georgie. I need to clean your bedroom... **WOW**, it really does stink in here! Have you trumped?!" his mum asked.

GEORGIE PANICKED.

His mum would find his trump jars!

As he was getting ready for school, he had an idea of how to get rid of his trump jars. He would simply throw them away in a bin outside his school!

He pulled them out from under his bed, shoved them into his school bag and hoped his mum wouldn't look inside.

Once his mum had dropped him off, he planned to run and throw the jars into the bin, then go into school.

No one would ever know about his trump jars.

Georgie wasn't sure why he had yelled stop.

His trump jars were gone.

"YIPPEE!"

He turned to run back into school, but the Headteacher had seen what had happened.

"Georgie, are you ok?" the Headteacher asked.
"I saw the robber steal your bag. We need to phone the police!"

Quite quickly a policeman arrived and asked what had happened.

"Oh, I see," said the policeman.
"We have been trying to catch this robber for a while, but he's just too quick for us. We don't know how to catch him."

Georgie didn't care.
He was just happy that his trump jars were gone and he wouldn't get in trouble with his mum.

The robber had run home.

It was the fifth school bag he had stolen that week.

It was just too easy. This bag was full to the top and he couldn't wait to see what was inside.

He put his hand in and slowly pulled out three jars.

"Wow, I hope these are all full of money!" he exclaimed.

He opened the jars and peered into them.

The smell from the jars quickly filled the room.

"**URRRGGHHHH**," the robber shouted.

"What is that disgusting smell?"

The robber couldn't breathe.

He ran outside to get away from the ghastly pong and rushed straight into a policeman.

"Well, well, well, what's happening here then?" said the policeman.

"Help me! That is the worst smell ever. **URRRGGHHHH**,

I robbed a school bag and it has the worst smell in the world in it. Please just take me away from it. It smells like hundreds and hundreds of trumps!"

And with that, the ghastly robber passed out on the street.

Once he awoke, the policeman arrested the robber and rang the school to inform them what had happened.

The school held an assembly and asked Georgie to come up to the front.

"Well done, Georgie. The police have caught the robber all because of your trump jars."

All the children were staring at him. He started to blush, but then they all started singing…

"Hip, hip, hooray, Georgie's trumps have saved the day!

Hip, hip, hooray, Georgie's trumps have saved the day!"

Georgie was happy that his trumps had helped catch the robber, so he decided the best thing to do right now was to turn around, put his bottom in the air and, as a thank you, he did a massive...

TRUMP!

www.ingramcontent.com/pod-product-compliance
Lightning Source LLC
Chambersburg PA
CBHW041122070526
44584CB00002B/242